Vortex

John W. Sexton

 DOGHOUSE

Vortex
is published by
DOGHOUSE
P.O. Box 312
Tralee G.P.O.
Co. Kerry
Ireland   Tel: +353 (0)66 7137547   email: doghouse312@eircom.net

April, 2005

ISBN 0-9546487-6-5

Edited for DOGHOUSE by Noel King

Cover illustration: Abeyant III. Oil on canvas. (c) Ailbe Collins. www.ailbe.com

Printed by Tralee Printing Works, Denny Street, Tralee

*Further copies available at 12 euro, post free, from the above address, cheques etc.
payable to Doghouse. Details of other DOGHOUSE books also available on request.*

Doghouse is a non-profit taking company, aiming to publish the best of literary works
by Irish born writers. Donations are welcome and will be acknowledged on this page.

For our 2005 publications, heartfelt thanks for donations from:

Tuatha Chiarraí   **Independent News & Media PLC**

Pauline Bewick; Bus Éireann; CH Chemists; Cill Rialiag Project; Tom Coffey;
Dr. Donal Daly; Dr. Pat English; ESB Networks; Mrs Norrie Gentleman;
William H. Giles & Co.; Hi Notes Music Co.; Donal Kelliher, Solicitor;
Kelliher's Hardware; Kelliher's Property Holding Co.; Kingdom Restaurants;
Liscahane Nurseries; Philip J. Manzor & Co.; Murphy, Ramsay, Walsh, Solicitors;
Florrie O'Carroll; Mr. Patrick J.F. O'Sullivan; Pierce & Fitzgibbon, Solicitors,
Mr. Paddy Prendergast; Stockbyte.

Dedicated to the memory of my brother

Gerard Sexton (1967 - 1985)

owl rips darkness
from the sky
the stars come through

The poems in this collection have previously appeared in:

The Burning Bush; Compost; The Cork Literary Review; The Illustrated Ape; Poetry Ireland Review; Poetry Scotland; The Shop; The Stinging Fly; The Stony Thursday Book.

Breacadh(Ed. Rosemary Canavan); Cúm(Ed. Moya Cannon); Heart of Kerry (Ed. Noel King); New Writing Cork 1999(Ed. Patrick Galvin); Or volge l'anno (Ed. by Marco Sonzogni, Dedalus Press); Podium 5(Ed. by Noel King); Poets For The Millennium(Ed. Ian Wild, Bradshaw Books).

The Ivory Tower, RTE; The Living Word, RTE; Rattlebag RTE; The Saturday Supplement, Radio Kerry; Spirit Level, RTE.

The Defeat of Destiny featured on the CD *Sons of Shiva*, with music by Hugh Cornwell.

Thanks to Seamus Hosey, to Poetry Ireland / Eigse Éireann and to The Royal College of Surgeons, Dublin for the launch of this book.

Special thanks to fellow poet Eileen Sheehan, whose comradeship and critique over the years have been a strength and inspiration. Thanks also to Magaret O'Shea and to the various members of The Fia Rua Writers' Group.

Let us find out, if we must be constrained,
Sandals more interwoven and complete
To fit the naked foot of Poesy:
Let us inspect the lyre, and weigh the stress
Of every chord, and see what may be gained
By ear industrious, and attention meet:
Misers of sound and syllable, no less
Than Midas of his coinage, let us be
Jealous of dead leaves in the bay wreath crown:
So, if we may not let the Muse be free,
She will be bound with garlands of her own.

from "If by dull rhymes our English must be chained"

John Keats

Contents

my secret witch

Her grey hair glitters under the moonlight
as she flies above the sea. Whales' fisted heads
part the waves below her. Storms fester
on the tip of her tongue. She seeds the air
with her presence and men turn in their sleep.
She is the nightmare of every child.
Women fear her for they fear they're her.
They're right to think that way. The woman
who falls asleep beside you is part of her dream.
She dreams that she flies above the earth, made
from the dreams of every woman who sleeps.
Sometimes she awakens in a strange place.
A frying pan is in her hand, egg
and sausages sizzling in fat. A child
is screaming in its cot and her husband
is shouting for no reason. Then she's
asleep again, storms festering on her tongue,
the nightmare of every child, every man's
suspicion of who his wife might be.

I know she is there, see her in the shot
of grey of my lover's hair. Await
the day when she stands before me in all
her magnificence, withers me with a single word,
and catching me by the ear
carries me high above the earth.

Mother, 1957

Mother pulled sea-grass from the fallen tide
and gathered shellfish in her aproned skirt;
she loosened scallions from the land to dry,
then picked fresh spuds behind her father's spade.
But in the secret earth of her own womb
the seed had burst and pushed towards the light,
and I became more living than the egg
that she would beat into the cake of brack.
O, milk had been spilled between her lover,
and soon harvest and feast would be over.

Vortex

My ten-year-old son is standing in the bath,
his body surrounded by an aura of steam;
bath-water runs down the spiked stalactites of hair
that crown his head. His blue eyes are incredibly bright,
but communicate no more than the water at his feet.

He is speaking a giggling song of invented words,
and I realise that he is mimicking the water,
for he has loosened the plug with his toe,
and the bath is turning in the vortex of its own substance,
sucking itself down into the foul sump beneath the house.

And now he is braying like a donkey,
for a dissolving lump of soap has caught in the plug-hole,
and the tune played by the bath
has changed to this raw screech.

I lift out the soap, and am surprised
that it seems alive with light, and for some reason
I am reminded of the soap created by Joseph Mengele
in the factories of Auschwitz. It was, from the accounts
of those who used it, a beautiful translucent soap,
made from the boiled remains of the murdered jews.

I lift my son from the bath and stand him on a towel.
He is quiet, no longer talking to the bath, for the bath is dry.
I rub his hair vigorously with a small towel;
he doesn't like it, but I persevere because it must be done.
I dry his body gently and am intrigued
that his skin has taken on some of the qualities

of the soap. Perversely, I am reminded once more
of Dr. Mengele. I remember a photograph I have seen
of him sitting in his office at Auschwitz-Birkenau.
On his desk is a lampshade, the twin of one
that he presented to the Feuhrer. It is made from human skin,
and I think,

   O Doctor Mengele, if my son was in your hands,
   what fine lampshade would you make of him?
   What cure would yours be,
   for the light that is smothered inside him?

   As I dry his arms and thighs
I see that the imprinted pattern of teeth-marks,
where he has bitten himself over and over again,
have begun to fade.
Being double-jointed, no part of his body is immune
from his teeth. His toes are raw,
where he has bitten the nails to the quick.

   As I clean the bath I send him into the hall
to put on his pyjamas. When I go out to him
he is lying on his back on the floor,
clapping the soles of his feet together,
applauding himself with his feet.

   O my silly son,
   where is it that you came from?
   Wherever it is,
   you brought yourself whole, as you are.

In the kitchen
I finish his hair with the dryer.
He takes hold of my waist and squeezes as tight as he can,
his fingers pinching my flesh.
Squeeze, he says, *Squeeze*.
Putting the dryer aside I loosen his fingers.
I lean down and kiss his head,
his wonderful clean hair,
but he is oblivious to my affection.

Later I check on my son in his bed.
He is fast asleep, his arms folded loosely over his head.
Mengele is standing at the far side of the room.
The hallway light from the crack in the door
slices through his body, swirls of dust are his only organs.
By his side, and along the sides of the bed,
I can see a half-circle of children, emaciated, their faces miserable.
Some are visibly retarded, some invisibly so,
but I can see what they are, know what they are,
have the space inside me that they fit.

Mengele gazes at my sleeping son, but he says nothing,
his face betrays nothing.
Only the children are talking, to themselves,
muttering incoherent mantras,
their voices like a vortex
drawing waters into unknown depths.

lon dubh

All those looking into the weed-choked weir
can hear your unmistakable warning.
You only sing when invisible, dressed
in the vibrant clothing of hedge or fern.
You wear the sharp briared floor like a hood.

When you were made your body was as clear
as glass. Then you flew into the evening
just a bit too far to come back. Darkness
tainted your body like smoke; night became
your colour and you stayed that way for good.

Now, they say, you never fly at night. Fear
hides you (even though you cannot be seen).
But during the day you're a dark blot, less
than light. Blackbird, every child knows your name.
Your voice takes on your shape inside the wood.

It is your thin *see see see* that I hear.
I enter the forest at your urging,
care nothing that my life is in a mess.
Night begins to fall but I'm glad I came.
Then darkness fills the space where once I stood.

Hedgehog Speaks

air is the element of the wasp;
but against the bent, tangled grasses
wasp is mine. its sting is nothing.
even the snake cannot escape my grasp.
humbler are the mouthfuls of beetles,
woodlice, snails. in the hedge i am king.
i trouble cattle in a way
so that milk drips from the teat,
and dig out the nests of mice, to eat
their blind defenceless young. only the flea
that roosts in my spines is god.

departure of the seven selves

Hanging in the wardrobe are the naked skins of seven bodies. I take them out one by one and lay them on the bed. I try one on and stand in the narrow hall, but the person in the mirror isn't me.

Back in the bedroom three of the flimsy bodies are missing, their hangers empty on the bed. The bedroom window is open and I glance into the garden. By the time I turn around the other three are gone as well.

I hear the front door slam but when I step into the front yard there is no one in sight.

Wearing the last remaining body I stand in the narrow hall, and although the person in the mirror isn't me I decide to keep it on.

Somewhere outside are six strangers, their empty bodies a perfect fit for anyone to hand.

Days later there is a knock on my door and six naked men are standing outside.

One of the men is full of hedge-birds, one is full of snails, one is full of shadow, one is full of sunlight, one is full of rain, one is full of fallen fruit.

Come with us, they say, and I follow. The sky is like a sheet of pale silk. I am amongst complete strangers, but we hold hands and walk ankle-deep into the wet grass.

Behind us the house shutters itself. There is no need to return.

Alter Ego

When I was a child I invented things
hidden in cupboards, asleep in the folds
of curtains; I heard the secret breathings
of a woman's voice in my head, a mould
that grew swollen, erupting into spores
that infected my imagination.
She lived in the dark space beneath the stairs,
and often possessed the television,
by which means she could talk to me for hours.
Mum and Dad couldn't see through her disguise,
were never aware that the house had claws
or that it resonated with her voice.
Through time she came together in my skin,
became my bones, blood, everything within.

The Legend Of Sylvia Plath

Raspberries leave their stain against his fingers
as my son pulls the fruit
from their collapsing scaffolding of sticks.
He is unaware of the wasps
gathering in their palaces of paper.
Dimensions of light filter into the garden,
and I think of Sylvia Plath
and her poems of bees,
the urge to write as if an internal hive
is erupting in frenzy,
the Queen Bee astride the smoking temple of wax,
the winged alter ego leaving her city of selves.
But it is October
and the raspberries have rotted
in a summer of rain,
my son's fingers were never stained,
and the image is merely a device
that poets use to get things going,
to discern the pivot
which balances lies and truth.

Annunciation

Mary had fallen, drawn into sleep
by the pages of her prayer-book.
And the television also dozed
into a grey, hissing haze of snow.
When she woke an hour later
the television was a square angel
of light, pulsing in the blue darkness,
its voice the soft vocabulary of snakes
telling Mary it had implanted
its electrical sperm in her brain.
She did not understand a word it said,
but unplugged it, rendering it dead.
In Heaven, though, the ghost of the T.V.
sat at the right hand of God
pondering at the thing it had begot.

Frogspawn

I pulled them, dull, insensate, from the pond,
their black yolks a blind many-eyed mass. Light
shone through the jar, charged the transparent womb
of trembling jelly, but failed to penetrate
those dark eggs.
               Left on top of the wardrobe
by next morning they had sprouted like beans.
Three more days and they had tails and whiskers
and congregated on the jar's glass floor.
I put the jar to my ear, imagined
their urgent gossip.
               A breath could disturb
the surface of their world, and I would watch
as they scattered to nowhere, their esses
of tails waving them forwards through water
that contained no possibilities.
               That
day I poured them into a fishbowl, placed
it on top of the bookcase and waited.

Waited as I wait now for them to grow
large enough to pour back into the pond.
After that I know they will be taken
into the mouths of fish and birds.
               Although,
no doubt, some will become frogs, get eaten,
again by birds, or sported to death by cats,
or scissored by the teeth of lawn-mowers.

Or lay eggs of their own, that come to this.

Uncle Aney, Granny, Mum & The Man Of Soot

A man made of soot lived in the long nose
of the chimney. At night, when turf collapsed
into ashes, he would come down and walk
through the kitchen. Every morning Granny
would mop up his footprints before we woke.
No one ever saw him except Aney,
who said he breathed into children's faces
and gave them bad dreams. So, after I woke
three nights in a row with the man of soot
just gone from the room, Mum took a bucket
and threw water on the embers. They hissed
a violent shaft of steam that stung our eyes,
but Granny said it chased the man of soot
right up the chimney and out of the house.

notes towards a tale of wonder

A child falls from a tree and is impaled through the heart by the spiked railings surrounding a churchyard.

No one dares remove the child's body from the railings until an ambulance has arrived, just in case there is a chance that he can survive. His body hangs limply outside the church, his mother is inconsolable. The priest stands powerless. A cat stops momentarily to sniff at the pool of blood accumulating on the pavement.

The child has no idea that his ruptured body is still caught on the railings. To his mind he is still falling. He fell clean through the railings, through the ground, through rock as yielding as soft toffee until he came to a ball of light. Now he is siphoned through a funnel of light; light so palpable that it is like a thick, clear treacle.

The child's falling comes to a gentle stop. He lands easily on his feet and discovers that he is standing in wet marshland, a low fog covering him as high as his waist. He cannot see his feet but can feel his shoes squelching into mud, can feel water seeping through his socks.

Eventually the fog clears but the ground becomes increasingly unstable until he is wading through watery mud. Soon he emerges into clear water; the water is up to his waist and at his feet he can see a shingled riverbed, for he is standing in the estuary of a great river.

Fish as large as seals appear beside him, their bodies speckled with gold and silver. They swim at either side of him, low against the shingle, their tails sweeping the floor of the estuary.

The water deepens but he continues to wade. Further and further behind him are the marshlands and before him is the open sea. Suddenly one of the fish slips between his legs and takes him on its back. He leans forward, the palms of his hands against the fish, its touch warm and metallic.

The fish gathers speed and he is forced to lean further into its back. The fish begins to dive and down he goes with it.

Now the water is like light, like the thick light he has fallen through earlier. All about him are thousands upon thousands of gold and silver fish, their bodies intense and glorious. Transcendent is he in an ocean of light.

Starlings sweep through the darkening sky. The churchwarden takes a hacksaw and begins to remove the spikes from the churchyard railings.

staining the eaves

Out in the backyard I open the tin.
I peer inside but nothing can enter
into the glop. Not even the ripe sun
that burns overhead. Quick Drying Woodstain
says the tin. Peering over my shoulder,
vainly hoping for a way to sneak in,
the sun considers its own reflection.
Soon I'm painting, high up on the ladder,
and the eaves are transformed from the bristles:
soaking up woodstain, the timbers darken.
Outdone, the sun sulks, steams amongst thistles.

the butcher's daughter

You and your father
are the only living things
behind the counter.
Tenderly you arrange
the remains
of his dedicated slaughter.

Your father is chopping sirloin
into precise slices.
Nothing is wasted.

From the corner of my eye
I see the blade of the cleaver.
For a brief moment I imagine
that he is disposing
of your last suitor.
You lay sausages on a tray,
folding them back on each other
by their strings, one by one,
like rows of unmentionable trophies.

Next you display some hearts
under a glass window.
The smallest of which,
on the left-hand corner,
is mine.
You brush it gently with a finger.
A shiver runs through my body.
Then you look up
into my eyes, and you know.

Cheng Yun-Sou Under Sorrow Bridge

The peony loosens its tightened buds
and the sound of petals I imagine
shifting against petals, is the chafing
of sheets against your skin. The song of birds
is your pillowtalk. The soft clash of heads
as the grass delights in assignation,
enticed by the breeze to show its passion,
taunts me with thought of you in other beds
but mine. Yet I know what I cannot see
standing in the stream for the flood's leaven
beneath this bridge to cleanse away my hurt.
I will wait here till water swallows me,
the river bursts and rises to Heaven;
till the moon's a hook from which hangs my heart.

ballad of the long-haired girl

the long-haired girl who travelled the world
to find herself, to find herself
what did she find on the horn of the moon
but a man supping from an ivory spoon
his head ablaze with yellow light
and he said I'm not the one

the long-haired girl who travelled the world
to find herself, to find herself
what did she find at the river's bed
but a fish-eaten man a long time dead
three gold rings upon each hand
and he said I'm not the one

the long-haired girl who travelled the world
to find herself, to find herself
what did she find behind the door
but a man lying upon the floor
his hair growing into the ground
and he said I'm not the one

the long-haired girl who travelled the world
to find herself, to find herself
what did she find at the garden's edge
but a man weaving a cloak of sedge
seven toes upon each foot
and he said I'm not the one

the long-haired girl who travelled the world
to find herself, to find herself
what did she find under the lid
but a man who was no longer hid
everything there and nothing gone
and he said I am the one

the long-haired girl who travelled the world
to find herself, to find herself
what did she find there and then
but the world was full of useless men
and none would do for a long-haired girl
so she said you're not the one

grave of the unknown cat

Because I was known to be fond of cats
my father-in-law gave me the task
of burying the dead stray that he had found
in the rush-choked field below the house.
In the evening, under the fading light,
I took the stiffened body and dug a tight
square hole. Into it went the cat, and in
the weakening daylight the hole caved-in
with shadows. I added a few scoops from the spade,
and the following year and in the years to come
watched as the place was finally covered
with the lush swords of feileastram.
And through that graveyard every spring
comes every neighbour's tom. Nods
a torn ear to the dead, then moves on.

Geasa

I am dreaming out loud
and my grandfather's face is a withered apple.
He sends me to fetch water
and the light is spilling through the trees.
I swing the enamelled bucket
into the streamers of light
but cannot catch them.

I walk through the limp grass
to the end of the sloping field
and lay the bucket on its side.
Sliding the flagstone to the edge
I look into the cold lens of the well.
Below me is a frog,
its body magnified through the water.
Though I break the surface with the bucket
the frog is unconcerned.

Still later the frog will visit me in dreams
perhaps for drinking from the bucket
or perhaps merely for catching sight of him

or perhaps it is simply
coming through the damp grasses of sleep
that the frog chances upon me unawares
and before I know it
I am dreaming out loud.

sonnet to the goddess of words

You led me to a room inside your head,
and feeling drowsy I lay down and died.
You told me that I was not really dead,
but no shouting could arouse me: You lied.
I had a bag of omens, from my Mum,
with whose magic I would be unsmothered:
a bee, a golden hair, a chrysanthemum.
The bee had flown, the hair grey, the flower withered.
And even the heavy sweater my Mammy knitted,
unravelled on a protruding, rusty nail,
and all those years of learning I regretted,
my apprenticeship to you of no avail.
I cannot wake up, but can only tread
stealthily, and rewind the unwound thread.

Birthright

The sky was bright and could fit exactly
inside my head, for the whole world was mine.

I was ten years of age and the crowned king
of thistles. With a sceptre of bamboo,
which Granda had given me, I sliced down
all those thistle princes in the bad fields.

Ah, John Sexton, boy, ye haven't killed them,
ye've only given birth. Ye've sent them off
to make more thistles beneath the ground. Yes,
I was the king of thistles, the world was mine.

A Letter To The King Of Ireland's Daughter

I dreamt
that your bed fell down the stairs.
Your husband was fast asleep,
tied in by the sheets,
and thus he slipped into a gaping hole
that had opened up by the front door.

At that point, disguised as a kitten,
I came into the house from the back garden,
and the garden was choked
as high as the bedroom windows
with grass.

You came into the kitchen,
naked except for your hair
which wreathed your body like a gown.
You picked me up by the loose flesh of my neck,

and as I hung from your hand
I could see my tail
curling hopelessly between my legs.
With a determined swing
you threw me back
into the swaying grasses of the garden.

By the time I returned to the house,
the house was gone,
and I could see you
pushing it down the street
on castors.

From his bed, wedged in the centre of the earth,
your husband was calling your name.
You were off to find him,
the long way round the world.
And the wind stirred at the grass
which also began to call:
puss, puss, puss

game of the sacrificed lovers   *(for twenty-four players)*

twenty-four people are in the garden, two are hidden.

one is hidden as the bud of a rose,
one is hidden as a blade of grass.

five young men stand to the east,
with five more pretending to be thrushes.

five young women stand to the west,
with five more pretending to be finches.

out of the mouths of the five young men fly the five pretending thrushes.
out of the mouths of the five young women fly the five pretending finches.

someone with dark skin pretends to be the king.
someone with pale skin pretends to be the queen.

the pretending king sends the pretending thrushes to search for a rose.
the pretending queen sends the pretending finches to fetch blades of grass.

five roses are brought to the pretending king.
five blades of grass are brought to the pretending queen.

the pretending king peels the petals from every rose.
the pretending queen curls the grass between her fingers.

the five pretending thrushes fly out to the east
followed by the pretending king and his five young men.

the five pretending finches fly out to the west
followed by the pretending queen and her five young women.

the rose trees begin to fade.
the grass begins to wither.

the garden is emptied of life.

In My Twelfth Year

At the bottom of our North London garden was a plum tree.
Each year it would yield a crop of three bitter plums.
Behind the tree, beyond the boundary of our garden,
was an alley-way, overgrown with thistles and briars,
which ran between the gardens of the street
that stood back to back with ours.

It was there, in the summer of 1970,
that my nine-year-old brother Martin, and myself,
found the angel. The angel was lying, wedged awkwardly
between the parallel rows of garden fences,
along the length of the alley. His head was as large
as a van, and was twisted painfully, so that his enormous face
was turned upwards towards our garden.
We looked down at him from the branches of the plum tree.

I fell down the back-stairs of Heaven, he said,
before blood began seeping from the corners of his mouth.
And until he finally closed them, we could see ourselves reflected
in his watering eyes.

Despite Martin's protests that it was too dangerous,
I climbed over the top of our rotting wooden fence, and stood
on the angel's face. But because of the gradient of the cheekbones
I had to crouch forwards so I wouldn't fall.
I gazed into the angel's nostrils:

I can't see anything, it's all hairy inside, I called,
and my voice echoed through the chambers
of the angel's nose.

I climbed higher up the angel's face
and pulled out one of his eyelashes. I began swishing it
through the air like a stick, and it thrummed resonantly.

As I stepped between the ridges
of the angel's brow, I could see that his wings
were crushed against the weight
of his body, and the alley was littered
with scattered feathers. I picked one out
from the tangle of his hair
and it was as large as a kite. I threw it into the air,
where it caught the warm summer current
and floated upwards, higher than all the houses.
    Let's get Dad, said Martin.

When Dad came out to the garden
the angel had gone. Dad stood on the groaning timbers
and surveyed the alley-way. That weekend
he erected a tall fence made from sheets of corrugated iron.
    You'll see no more angels now, he said.

The blue-skinned witch

The blue-skinned witch is as dark as a sloe.
She stands on the wavering edge of shadows,
waiting for the innocent to wander
close to her place. They'll never see her, just
feel a cold rush of air touch their faces.
Then they're caught for good by the blue-skinned witch.

So confused they hardly know which is which,
they eat thistles for cabbage, bite a sloe
thinking it an apple. Watch their faces
next time you visit them in the shadows.
Deadened from eating bitter things, they just
sit there pulling faces, never wander

from the place they're trapped, will never wander
till the day they die. All the time the witch
will be preparing a bed for you, just
in case you decide to stay. Don't. One sloe
will fur your tongue for good, install shadows
forever inside your head; makes faces

at any fool who eats it. Makes faces
at the curious eaters who wonder
what one will taste like. They taste like shadows
which have been fermented for months. The witch
takes advantage of this fact, knows a sloe
will keep all those fools dull, sluggish. Not just

for a few months, but forever. Not just
forever, but as long as clocks have faces.
That's her favourite saying. *Clocks don't go slow
in Eternity* is another. No wonder
she catches fools. Who'd tell her for a witch,
this humorous old lady? The shadows

for starters; and the souls trapped in shadows.
This is not a world for the good or just.
For this world belongs to the blue-skinned witch.
No stamps in *her* stamp-album. Just faces.
So, next time be careful where you wander.
And, till the first frost, never eat a sloe.

Never tread on shadows, avoid faces
you don't know. Just be safe: *never* wander.
The blue-skinned witch is as dark as a sloe.

A Spider Repairing Its Web

lifted my brother to see
window above kitchen door
on the outside where spider
laboured its tattered web
crashed upon, pollen-seed fluff
caught now and then by the wind
and rattled against the glass
feather-ruffling the spider's home
who scrambled to tackle the radial spires
bunching together a few at a time
pollen's spokes tied with a ribbon of web
completed cut and dislodged
so could chart new spider-line
to gauge exact position of stars
from kitchen's primitive lens

Song Of The Restless Gypsy

he woke from a dream of a golden coin as large as the moon
and the moon shone down on his sleepy-eyed face
so he said to himself, he said to himself, the moon is mine
so he left his house with the doors ajar and the moths came in to eat the light
and down by the river he stood on the back
of the drowning woman with her hair afloat
and she took him down to the mouth of the sea
and the moon shone down on his sleepy-eyed face
so he said to himself, he said to himself, the moon is mine

then three white fishes came out of the brine
and one said yes and one said no and one said we shall see
so he followed the fishes into the depths,
one for yes, one for no and one for maybe
and the ocean's wet tongue it slobbered him whole
and it filled his mouth and it filled his head
and the moon shone down on his sleepy-eyed face
so he said to himself, he said to himself, the moon is mine

come down come down to my bed of sand
said the drowning woman to the drowning man
but he said my love I surely can't for tonight I dreamt of the moon above
and I've left my house with the doors ajar
and I've followed three fishes to the ocean's floor
but I'll give you a kiss and maybe two
and when I've gone you can whisper my name
and the moon shone down on his sleepy-eyed face
so he said to himself, he said to himself, the moon is mine

and the drowning woman pushed him away
and her tears swelled up and filled the bay
and up he floated on his back and broke the surface with a slap
and seagulls came and pecked his skin
and fishes came up and nibbled his flesh
and some said yes and some said no and some said we shall see
and the moon shone down on his sleepy-eyed face
so he said to himself, he said to himself, the moon is mine

then he came to the beach with the clattering stones
washed up with seaweed, sticks and bones
and a woman came down with her hair aflame
and stood on his chest and whispered his name
and she said young man I'm leaving this place
for I dreamt last night of a golden coin
and the moon shone down on her sleepy-eyed face
so she said to herself, she said to herself, the moon is mine

Old tobacco tins

The ghosts of flaked tobacco lingered
in those empty tins for years. I'd keep
some in the toy-box, often fingered
open the lids to let the scent seep
into the room, so the ghosts could walk
at their ease, their sharp aroma nip
my nose. Then I would snap the lids back
so they'd be trapped again. Other kids
had no time for captive smells, would check
different guests into theirs. Like maggots
for instance, the perfect fishing bait.
On the riverbank I'd watch song-birds
hovering over the churning grubs, wait
to see them peck those throbbing gems
and fly off. Wasps would also raid
those tins, lift a maggot and be gone.

Along the sun-glared river the tins shone.

If I could make the perfect verse

If I could make the perfect verse I would:
golden pheasants would peck upon your lawn
and all good things would happen as they should.

I'd give you fair dreams boxed in sandalwood
and all the terrors of the night would drown.
If I could make the perfect verse I would.

The hooded crow would lose his dreary hood.
All kings and queens would answer to the pawn
and all good things would happen as they should.

Silver into gold, bad would turn to good,
monsters would put aside their tasks and yawn.
If I could make the perfect verse I would.

No one would ever be misunderstood.
Night would shorten, surrender to the dawn
and all good things would happen as they should.

Instead, poems have withered where they stood
or choked inside the tightened womb, unborn.
If I could make the perfect verse I would
and all good things would happen as they should.

I Am A Poem Of Nightingales

(i)
The sliding disc of the nightingale's eye
is a dark siphon of light.

(ii)
The king unscrewed his forehead
to release a dream of nightingales.

(iii)
The nightingale has no time for the open sky,
preferring the thorny labyrinth of the hedge.

(iv)
Do I prefer this silence
or the nightingale's warning that I am here?

(v)
In the city of Heresy
mechanical nightingales sing hosannas of rust.

(vi)
The nightingale's tumbling notes are unfathomable
to my ear as sense. To me it is only music.
The nightingale keeps his secret.

(vii)
The nightingales fly in enormous circles.
Am I at their centre, or do they fly
to keep me out of something greater?

(viii)

The black hearse circled his home one last time,
before taking him to the grave.
The earth that fell on his coffin
was the colour of nightingales.

(ix)

The mystery of the nightingale
is twenty-one words in the dictionary.

(x)

Using his window-sill as a table
nine-year-old Beethoven
transcribed the song of the nightingale.

(xi)

No nightingale can be heard
when the river is shouting.

(xii)

Night lasts forever,
and the snow is white in the darkness.
I am the eternal moment of the nightingale.

The Spirits Of The Dead

On the edge of the road the carcass of a fox
has been flattened by passing cars. Two magpies
are troubling the crushed pelt for meat. As I pull in
they rise majestically, like two angels,
their pied bodies magnificent in the morning light.

I leave the car-door ajar and walk along the road
to the dead fox. His innards are spilled everywhere,
his body separated from his head, and his face is pressed flat
into the black gravel, the skull pulverised into nothing.
With a dead stalk of bramble I prise his face from the road.

Hanging by its ear it is a rancid mask.
With a flick of my wrist I send the fox's face
through the air. It comes to rest amongst the branches
of hazel that hedge the road. Framed against the leaves,
looking down at me, it is utterly perverse.

Returning to the car I drive on to Portmagee. The journey
takes over an hour, but I remember nothing of it.
Down by the boats a fisherman agrees to take me to the Skellig.
We have to wait for a coach-load of German tourists.
Within five minutes of setting off they are throwing up.

At the Skellig I detach myself from the others.
I have a sudden feeling that I have forgotten something
and realise that I should have brought the face
of the dead fox. This seems absurd, but I am shadowed
by the conviction that I should have brought it with me.

Sitting by a heap of fallen rocks I read of the legend
of Ana Ní Áine. That's the one about the dark cloud
that smothers a boatload of day-trippers. Inside the cloud is the spirit
of a woman. She has murdered several people, including her own child.
A priest travelling on the boat absolves her of her sin and the cloud dissolves.

The spirit of the woman is released, and the boat travels on unmolested.
I am reading the story out loud. The German tourists are wondering
what the hell I am doing. A raven begins cawing from a spike of rock.
On the mainland the fox's face is still hanging from the hazels.
Suddenly I feel worthless, knowing I missed the chance to set him free.

After the Argument

I can't stand another moment
of these kids, this fucking house or.you,
pierce her armed words like the thorns from roses
as I stand in the garden idly plucking at bushes,
kindling this fire of talk in my head.
Then a buzz, the sound of another's anger,
the vicious whirr of a wasp,
plunging its brutal sting into the body
of a fly to which it clings; tumbling wildly,
the fly and wasp both prisoners
of the one's controlling grasp.
Her words integrate this insect struggle
as I flounder confused, as if still drunken
with anger, suffused with my own venom.

A Unicorn Addresses The Queen Of The Darkened Meadow

One moment I was not, and then I was.
I formed in the silver tresses of hair
that spilled from the moon. Dew
was my flesh as I rose from the furze.
My body was shuddering water, my flanks
rippled like the sly treacherous river
that calls the saddened lover to its edge.
From my crown sprouted a twisted horn
that could sever the sky. But your daughter
didn't cry. She laughed. I was the horse
of light, that travelled seven leagues through night
and brought her through the regions of the dead
to the safe green fields inside her head.
But the moon drew me back to where I'd come.
Your daughter woke. The moon slept. And I was gone.

My Father's Journey

I remember, in the orange light
of the lamp, our shadows throbbing
against the walls, looking into the white
marbled face of my father. He'd been dead

for three days, yet now was scraping
the thick bristles of his beard
with the ivory-handled razor. *You see
this razor*, he said, *it was with a blade*

*as sharp as this that your uncle Olavur
sliced me out from that whale's stomach.
They'd thought I'd drowned, but there
I was, asleep in the middle of a whale.*

He'd been missing for three days,
presumed drowned, just one more body
slipped from a whaler. No one knew
that beneath the ship he'd been siphoned

into the grey hulking mouth of a whale.
On the third day this same creature
had been harpooned, its body dragged
into the slicing-bays. It's thick skin,

troubled by sea-lice, was pulled back
from the blubber, and uncle Olavur cut open
the long gut. Inside he found his brother,
floating in the juices of the stomach.

As they lifted him out
he began to stir, like a man disturbed
in his bed. The acid of the whale's gut
had bleached his skin to the colour

of a candle, and he stayed that way
for three years, till the day he fell,
for the final time, into the sea.
His body was never found, but uncle Olavur

swore that he looked for him
inside every whale he gutted.
And I cried every night
for three months after he went.

I cried for three months
until one night, in the month
of August when the moon was full,
I dreamt I was at sea, just like

when the black sky is sealed tight
from horizon to horizon
and you can sense the sea's grey skin
itching beneath the boat.

But as I looked down at my feet
I saw that I was not standing
on the deck of a boat, but on a whale,
barnacles crottled to its flesh.

I could see the whale's eye,
not dim as their eyes really are,
but as round and bright as a porthole.
As I gazed into it I could see my father,

just like gazing through a window.
He was standing on a ladder
and waving. He was waving goodbye.
Then the whale submerged

and I was left floating in the sea.
When I woke up, the moon
still piercing the bedroom window,
I knew that my father was still alive,

that he would live forever, wandering
through the green corridors of the ocean.

He works in the shadow factory

He works in the shadow factory, turning the valves of the enormous tank. He watches the negative tons of raw shadow through the safety of a porthole.

On the way to the works canteen he passes the assembly-line. Thousands of aerosols full of shadow rattle along the conveyor belt.

It is the middle of summer, the factory's busiest time. The aerosols are stamped with the warning: FOR DAYTIME USE ONLY

From the canteen window he sees trucks leaving the factory gates. As he glances at his newspaper he notes the latest public concern.

A spokesman for the factory is quoted in the paper. The spokesman says that shadows occur routinely in nature: *Even a newborn baby has a shadow.*

After work he places his overalls into the mouth of an incinerator; before leaving the building he washes in the communal shower.

He works in the shadow factory, turning the valves of the enormous tank. At night he sleeps with the light on, all the shadows of the room in their rightful place.

the key of heaven

The key of heaven is a small black book.
Open it at any page and doorways
will open into oceans and heavens,
hells and purgatories. Gold-skinned lions
will meet you teeth to flesh. You'll die and live
and die again. Jesus will offer you
blood, the Devil bread. Gods, eyes in their hands,
will touch your brow and read your thoughts. Angels
will peel away your seven skins, breathe them
into life and peel new skins in turn. You,
a myriad of yourself, universe
of all the universe can hold, will fall
and let fall the book. With a start you'll wake.
Open it. Open it at any page.

Mothra

light a lantern to catch my soul
lure me from my palace of rice
from the bearded grasses call me out
shout shout shout shout

my name fills the throats
of children
calling from their cots
              the first word they have
              before mammy, before daddy
              before heaven, before God
              before angels, before devils
              before teddies, before dolls

my wings will bleed
              their golden dust
my shadow swallows meadow
              swallows shadow with its rust

i am the moth made up
of all your dreams
the times-tables
of your restless beds
i fill the night
with velvet wings
i am the blood
swelling in aching heads

first-born sons are caught
     in the stare
         of the toad with a hundred eyes
first-born daughters are less
     than the less
         of ghostflies
the three-day's child
     is dead in the hearse
         of the black-coated coffin-maker
the wheat is withered
     in the teeth
         of the hay-raker

i am summoned to battle the many deaths
     the monsters, the ogres
         the reeking Bad Breaths

i am the angel-guardian
     of the snivelling child
         of the infant bawling through snot
i am the moth-mind
     the fluttering collective of every moth

light a lantern to catch my soul
lure me from my palace of rice
from the bearded grasses call me out
shout shout shout shout

The Garden Of Eden Is Gone In The Head

the garden is lost in itself
its mind is a serpent in earth
guarding its fragments of delf
its body the shadows of birds

its mind is a serpent in earth
it dreams of an unbroken cup
its body the shadows of birds
covering the down from the up

it dreams of an unbroken cup
that an angel empties of stars
covering the down from the up
seeding the heavens of wars

that an angel empties of stars
which the serpent stole before time
seeding the heavens of wars
and cracking the cup at its rim

which the serpent stole before time
let fall from the grip of its lips
and cracking the cup at its rim
watched as it all became bits

let fall from the grip of its lips
this vessel that now was no more
watched as it all became bits
the was that is after before

this vessel that now was no more
guarding its fragments of delf
the was that is after before
the garden is lost in itself

On An August Night The Sea Reclaims Its Own

The sea was awake,
sleeplessly grinding its teeth.
And although warned
that it was a thief,
and would steal the breath
of those who went too near,
nevertheless she chanced
to go there. She could hear
the water mutter
its incessant troubles,
scattering its thoughts
amongst consonants of pebbles,
and as she ventured
by the stars' weak light
to the very edge of the pier,
midnight aged one minute
and she could hear the water call her:
...*daughter, daughter, daughter*...

The Wildlife Of London, 1970-1971

When kids brought jam-jars full to the brim
with green slimy water and frogs-born
for the teacher to see what they had got
I can still remember the sheer wonder
and the jealous urge to know
where in the car-clotted streets
frogs could be got.

I was twelve before I realised
that it was frogspawn not frogs-born
but I kept the word in my head
like a secret.
That summer Paul Cain
took me to the quarry at Arnos Grove.
We cut through Arnos Park
and crossed the shallow river to Pymmes Green.
Surrounded by the crumbling
quarry walls, that trickled stone by stone
into the weed-choked pond
I felt that I was in the middle of the country.
Over there's the main road and the box-works,
but ya wouldn't know it, would'ja?

No, you wouldn't know it.
You wouldn't know either
that the water was thick with newts
that you could entice with the ripple of your fingers.
We brought them home in jam-jars.
They were dead in a week.
It's the tap-water, son,
said Dad. *It's got lime in it.*
Kills them dead. It's rainwater you want
for those boyos. Rainwater.

The summer ended and the rainwater came
but too late for the newts. One afternoon
while looking at the twisting sheets
of rainwater from my bedroom window
I spotted clusters of ladybirds
crammed together beneath the window sill.

In a book I read that they were hibernating
and would emerge the following summer.
But the following summer they were dead,
their bodies tarnished with fungus.
I picked them out with a penknife,
and cast the brittle husks from the opened window.
I was thirteen.

Roland gets it

Martin Marky had traded a headbutt
in the school-yard, just because Roland was smart.
Roland's head began to grow a turnip,
swelling its way over his skull through Maths
and even into History. *I don't*
like the look of that, said his mother. *That's*
what you get for fighting. Sit down and rest.
And don't fall asleep. Are you dizzy? Is
there a headache with it?

                        Yes, mum. I know,
mum. I will, mum. I won't, mum. No, mum. Yes,
mum, said Roland. In the living-room, plonked
down on the sofa, he began to die.
On the telly they were doing King Lear.
Roland watched through pain, felt the telly suck
him into itself. An old man croaked out
a song. And the song became real. Became
Roland. The turnip exploded into
pulp. Roland was everywhere at once. Coal
was shovelled into his mouth. The factories
of England smothered the countryside thick
with smoke. Winston Churchill gave the order
to bomb Berlin with anthrax. But first they
had to make the bomb; then he changed his mind.
Roland was astride an ebony horse,
dressed in armour oiled in blood. He rode through
a forest. Everything was totally
fucking mad. The ebony horse took him
fast as a breath up to the wooden gates
of a tower. Roland put a trumpet to his lips

and began to blow. The tower fell down
and squashed Roland flat. Fuckit anyway
didden ee blod id ollup an is ed
filled yup wiv th'yoll ov imman istree
ental ee fond imselv

               awakening

against the hillside grass. He rose, naked,
sloughing off sleep. A white horse, taking leave
of its chomping, clipped up hoof-fulls of earth
as it came to him. And he took himself
up on its back, and rode the steepening
slope, down towards the beginning of is

One of those days with your mother

Your mother stands in the kitchen weaving
beehives from straw. At first I think they're hats,
watch her arrange them on the floor in rows.
She's silent when I ask her what she's at,
so I say nothing else, assume it's work
she does to make ends meet. From the garden
bees begin to file in through a window.
They enter the hats and I realise
for the first time that she's making hives. Now
everything is beginning to make sense.
Until, that is, the hives become so full
of bees that each begins to move swiftly
across the kitchen tiles. I can't tell you
at which point they each turn into a cat,
but that's exactly what happens. And right
in the middle of all this chaos, calm
as could be, is your mother, still weaving
beehives from straw. I open the backdoor,
deciding it's best to let out the cats,
and step through to the garden. Bees rush in
and I walk out onto the lawn. A thrush
sings from his high perch. I look up and see
his stippled chest catching the sunlight. Bees
fill my head with their sound. A single dress
hangs from the washing line. Quite forgotten,
it's been there for days. Then something snags me
and I cannot move. So I glance around.
My shadow is caught in the garden fence.
Yes, your mother 's quite mad, but I love her.

Foxman *versus* The City Of The Men-Men

*for two voices

(1)

The pipe from the Misery Works leaks its greasy waste into the waters of the
canal. Its enormous chimneys smother the city with smoke. Pregnant women
with grey skin enter its gates at dawn.

(2)

**in-ferned-caverns-of-hidden-i   snout-into-cunt-of-vixen-mate   rutted-
fuck-becomes-withered-rut   earth-fuck-wetted-cunt-is-us**

(3)

The women are taken on trolleys to the delivery-rooms. Under general anaes-
thetic a tiny foetus is removed from each mother by caesarean section.

(4)

**burst-innards-from-worm-skin   blood-juiced-beetles-death-am-i
juices-of-blackberries-my-teeth-am-i   blooded-birthlings-my-teeth-
am-i**

(5)

The foetuses are washed and sorted, and taken to the canning plant. The finest
are placed in pickling jars, their umbilicals floating above them.

(6)

**scavanged-afterbirth-from-mothering-sheep   bloods-the-thirst-of-
thistle-tongue**

(7)

An ambulance the colour of smoke is parked in the factory forecourt. The driver, discarding his cigarette through the side window, glances at the embankment over the canal. A fox is moving through the scrub. The driver stares till it is out of sight.

(8)

with-spraint-of-piss-my-place-mark-i   canalside-sedge-and-cottongrass furzied-hill-and-briary-path

(9)

Women with grey skin form into queues outside the insemination rooms.

(10)

the-pups-are-weaned-on-disabled-mice   fox-is-yes

(11)

The jars of the pickled foetuses are exported to the continent. Those that are tinned are reserved for the home market. Packed into lorries, they are distributed to supermarkets. Unpacked in turn they are placed on shelves. Untutored in the voice, the stacked tins of the dead are voiceless.

displacing the inner place

It is the summer of 1967 and I am nine years of age. We've come over from
London for a holiday and we're staying at Mum's place in Brosna, which is in
North Kerry. We're staying in the house where my mother was born. My
Grandparents claim me as their own and there are uncles everywhere.
Eccentric uncles, cranky uncles, funny uncles, wise uncles, old uncles and
young uncles. It seems that for each day I have a different uncle who wants
to be my uncle. This uncle thing seems complicated and they appear inca-
pable of doing it all at once, but can only manage it one uncle at a time. At
least, that's how I tend to remember it. One uncle at a time.

As we leave the yard the damp thatch is steaming
in the morning sun, and the square field of barley
is shining like the lid of a golden tin.

We climb a gate into the untended land
behind the house. *Mind your step there, John Sexton,*
says Uncle Jimmy. He has come out to look for a finch.
He's going to teach it to sing My Darling Clementine,
and sell it for a hundred guineas at the fair.

*Watch out for frogs, John Sexton - they'll cover you
in warts*, says Uncle Jimmy, as we jump
a narrow stream. Beyond the water the land is humped,
fertile only for stones and furze.

There's a horse in your ear, says Uncle Jimmy,
cuffing me gently on the side of the head. Instantly
from my ear he pulls a half-crown. He turns it
in his fingers, and I see a picture of a horse
grazing on the face of the coin. *Put that in your pocket,
John Sexton*, says Uncle Jimmy.

We climb the first hill, picking our way
through paths that zigzag gorse. *There's seven crows.*
But don't look at them, John Sexton, or you'll be dead
in a week, says Uncle Jimmy.

He stops suddenly and dips his hands into the middle
of a furze bush. I lean close and see the small
yellow lanterns of startling flowers.

Out of the bush Uncle Jimmy pulls a trap, like a basket,
made of woven twigs. Inside is a wran, fluttering in panic.
Not your turn yet, says Uncle Jimmy, as he lets it out,
setting it free.

It flys urgently, in low scooping lines,
almost bouncing off the fists of furze that dot
the rough hilly ground.

I pull a thorn from a furze bush, and clean out
the soft black soot from beneath a finger-nail.
I am no longer a child.
Uncle Jimmy is standing in front of me,
his face creased from smiling. He's been dead,
and with the dead, for years. I can see
right through him.

I realise now that it is not simply the uncle, but the place. Uncle and place morph together, until they are inseperable.

Some people maintain that place is a state of mind. This sounds so reasonable when you say it out loud, that many believe it to be true. But I would rather believe that place is a state of being. That also sounds reasonable when you say it out loud, but I am not really sure if I even know what it means.

I was born on the 6th of May, 1958, of the small Irish Republic of my Mother's womb. As she was at that time in London, in a place called Newington Green, that is where I slipped out. The sea-doors were opened and I found myself disembarked in the wrong place.

It was as if the harbourmaster had negligently cut my cordage, to set me adrift beyond the safety of the shallow saltings and finally to the mercies of the tides.

Due to my confinement while travelling I arrived not only blind but incompetent in every limb. Furthermore, I was completely unlearned in the language of the people I now found myself amongst.

The vessel in which I travelled I came to know as Mother. And, although in our early years together she never travelled much beyond the confines of North London, she nevertheless managed to pick up four other stowaways, each one of which came out from their journey as blind and as incompetent in every limb as I had been.

Anyone who has persevered this far and is still reading may justifiably come to the conclusion that I am being facetious or smart. But the truth is that I not only sincerely believe my mother to be a place, but also a portal for those who come after her to step from the possibilities of one place to another. Not merely place, but the possibilities of place. What does this mean, possibilities of place?

Well, if I stand in my garden, the uncut grasses risen to my knees, my steps disturbing the courses of beetles, butterflies haphazardly crossing before me, then I am in a place. But if I dream that I stand in my garden, the uncut grasses risen to my knees, my steps disturbing the courses of beetles, butterflies haphazardly crossing before me, then I am in a possibility of place.

My parents remain in England. One of those stowaways I mentioned earlier, a younger brother, died some years ago in a car accident and he is buried in London. My mother refuses to retire home to Ireland because she believes that there would be no one willing to pray at his grave.

It would be untended. So my parents will never come home. My mother remains behind to pray at the grave of my brother. My brother's grave is a place to anchor my mother. But because I live here in Ireland, I can only be with my mother in possibilities of place. And these possibilities occur always in dreams. For instance.

My mother is in the kitchen. She is sitting at the fire, a zinc bath full of water on the floor at her feet. I hand her a tortoise. She prises open the shell with a blunt dinner knife, and she removes the creature that is inside. Although naked, it seems totally without concern, and she places it into the bath. As she starts to wash the naked tortoise it begins to grow, until finally it is the size of a man. We all look down at the empty shell, now impossibly small.

So far I have made no mention of my father. Unless of course I mentioned him earlier unbeknown to myself. This is a distinct possibility as I am a poet, and my father could have already appeared metaphorically. Metaphor is a common ailment amongst poets, and is not always easily spotted. Perhaps my father is the harbourmaster who slipped my moorings. Who is to know?

As with my mother, I am only with my father in *possibilities* of place.

I once dreamt that I had written a short story called *The Consciousness Of Discovered Objects*. The following morning I wrote out the entire story word for word:

A man lifts a flat stone in his garden. Underneath is the fragile husk of a chrysalis. The man sees that by moving the stone he has broken the chrysalis. Inside he finds a small replica of himself, naked and asleep. Naked and asleep, he dreams that he has become a small replica of himself. Waking, he emerges from the shattered husk to discover a father who has chosen him at random to be his son; and he begins to think, I am now myself and no longer him.

This is me with my father, in a possibility of place. Or perhaps my father is the possibility of place. Again, who is to know?

Yes, who is to know? Who is to know anything? People, places, possibilities of place?

My eldest son, Matthew, is in the garden, the unkempt grasses nearly risen to his waist. This is not a possibility of place. This is a place. It is real. My son is fourteen. He turns to look at me and he says Yes.

Yes, yes, yes says my son.

He is fourteen years of age, yet he has a language comprehension of three years and ten months. He is autistic and to him language is a nonsense.

I remember his first attempt at verbal communication when he was a child in my arms. We were in the front yard. The actual front yard, not the possibility of the front yard. In the high pines above the house crows were calling to each other. He began to call back to them, like a crow. Before long crows and child were talking between the high pines and the house, their voices resonating in chorus.

But today he is saying Yes.

Yes, Yes, Yes he says, and his Yes takes on the mantle of the garden, the grasses nearly risen to his waist. Everything is Yes. I take his hand and we stand together in the garden. In his kingdom of Yes.

The Defeat Of Destiny

On the night I was born
an owl crushed a mouse in its beak,
a fox stole a hen,
tadpoles slithered from their jellied eggs,
beetles were swallowed by silent birds,
ants laboured in their kingdom of soil,
as I forced open my mother's womb.
As the waters and blood gave way
the lizard adjusted beneath its stone,
the earwig destroyed the opening bud,
the weasel counted its hoard of bones,
a man mistook death for sleep,
a fish snapped at a drifting worm,
and I took my first uncertain breath.

John W. Sexton is a poet, dramatist, children's writer, broadcaster and radio scriptwriter. He was the creator and scriptwriter for RTE's children's radio show, **The Ivory Tower** which ran to 103 episodes. His novels based on this series, **The Johnny Coffin Diaries** and **Johnny Coffin School-Dazed**, are published by The O'Brien Press and have been translated into Serbian and Italian. His previous collections of poetry are **The Prince's Brief Career** (1996) and **Shadows Bloom / Scáthanna Faoi Bhláth**, with Irish translations by Gabriel Rosenstock(2004). Under the ironic pseudonym of Sex W. Johnston he has released an album with legendary Stranglers frontman Hugh Cornwell, entitled **The Sons Of Shiva** (Track Records).